Read-About® Holidays

# Thanksgiving

## By Trudi Strain Trueit

**Reading Consultant**
Cecilia Minden-Cupp, PhD
Former Director of the Language and Literacy Program
Harvard Graduate School of Education
Cambridge, Massachusetts

Children's Press®
A Division of Scholastic Inc.
New York  Toronto  London  Auckland  Sydney
Mexico City  New Delhi  Hong Kong
Danbury, Connecticut

Designer: Herman Adler
Photo Researcher: Caroline Anderson
The photo on the cover shows an American family enjoying their
Thanksgiving dinner.

**Library of Congress Cataloging-in-Publication Data**

Trueit, Trudi Strain.
  Thanksgiving / by Trudi Strain Trueit.
      p. cm. — (Rookie read-about holidays)
    ISBN-10: 0-531-12460-6 (lib. bdg.)       0-531-11841-X (pbk.)
    ISBN-13: 978-0-531-12460-4 (lib. bdg.)       978-0-531-11841-2 (pbk.)
    1. Thanksgiving Day—United States—History—Juvenile literature. I. Title.
II. Series.
  GT4975.T78 2007
  394.2649–dc22                          2006004432

CHILDREN'S PRESS, and ROOKIE READ-ABOUT®, and associated
logos are trademarks and/or registered trademarks of Scholastic Library
Publishing. SCHOLASTIC and associated logos are trademarks and/or
registered trademarks of Scholastic Inc.
1 2 3 4 5 6 7 8 9 10 R 16 15 14 13 12 11 10 09 08 07

Think of something you are thankful for. Is it your family or friends? How about lunch when you're hungry?

I am Thankful for...

Since ancient times, people have given thanks for their food. Festivals were held to celebrate the harvest in ancient Rome, China, and Egypt. A good harvest meant there would be plenty of food to last through the winter.

An ancient Egyptian painting celebrating the harvest in Egypt

The Pilgrims arriving at Plymouth

People from Europe began sailing to America in 1492. The Pilgrims were one of the first groups of English people to choose America as a new place to live.

The Pilgrims settled a town called Plymouth in 1620. Plymouth is in present-day Massachusetts.

The Pilgrims were not ready for their first long, cold winter in America. They did not have enough food. Many of them died before spring.

The Pilgrims at Plymouth

Native Americans knew that deer provided meat and skin for clothing.

Native Americans had lived in America for thousands of years. They knew what foods grew well there and had good hunting skills. They agreed to help the Pilgrims.

Native Americans showed the Pilgrims how to fish and hunt. They told them which plants were safe to eat. They taught them how to grow corn and other crops. The Pilgrims had never seen corn before!

A Native American woman planting corn

The first Thanksgiving

The Pilgrims had a good
harvest by the next fall.
They wanted to celebrate.
The Pilgrims invited
the Native Americans
to a feast.

They had duck, deer, fish, corn bread, boiled pumpkin, nuts, and berries. They may have eaten turkey, too.

The Native Americans and Pilgrims had plenty to eat.

# November 2007

| Sunday | Monday | Tuesday | Wednesday | Thursday | Friday | Saturday |
|--------|--------|---------|-----------|----------|--------|----------|
|        |        |         |           | 1        | 2      | 3        |
| 4      | 5      | 6       | 7         | 8        | 9      | 10       |
| 11     | 12     | 13      | 14        | 15       | 16     | 17       |
| 18     | 19     | 20      | 21        | 22       | 23     | 24       |
| 25     | 26     | 27      | 28        | 29       | 30     |          |

The celebration lasted three days. This was the first Thanksgiving in America. Nowadays, Thanksgiving is always held on the fourth Thursday of November in the United States.

Many other countries also have a holiday to give thanks for the harvest.

# Ways to Celebrate

Around the world, people often celebrate the harvest by gathering and sharing a meal. In Korea, it is the custom to serve rice cakes. People bake round, flaky pastries called moon cakes in China. This is to honor the full moon at harvest time.

A moon cake

Some of the foods included in a Thanksgiving meal

It is traditional to have a Thanksgiving feast in the United States. Families sit down to a meal of turkey, stuffing, potatoes, cranberry sauce, and pumpkin pie.

They may take turns saying what they are grateful for before they eat.

One family may go for a hike before dinner. Another family may play a game of touch football after their meal. Some families play indoor games.

A father and son playing touch football on Thanksgiving

Everyone loves the balloons in a Thanksgiving Day parade.

Many people relax after eating such a big dinner. They may watch football. Earlier in the day, some people watch a Thanksgiving Day parade on television. The balloon floats are huge!

Some people spend the holiday serving dinner to the poor. One family might take homemade pumpkin pie to elderly neighbors. Many feel the best way to give thanks is to share with others.

Helping feed other people is a good way to give thanks.

# Words You Know

feast

meal

moon cakes

Native Americans

30

parades

Pilgrims

Plymouth

touch football

# Index

## About the Author

Trudi Strain Trueit is a former television news reporter and weather forecaster. She has written more than thirty fiction and nonfiction books for children. Ms. Trueit lives near Seattle, Washington, with her husband Bill.

## Photo Credits

Photographs © 2007: AP/Wide World Photos: 3 (Joel Andrews/The Lufkin Daily News), 29 (Jeff Chiu), 26, 31 top left (Jeff Christensen); Art Resource, NY/ Erich Lessing: 5; Corbis Images: 6, 9, 14, 30 top left, 31 top right, 31 bottom left (Bettmann), 25, 31 bottom right (Chuck Savage); Getty Images/Ryan McVay/ Photodisc Green: cover; North Wind Picture Archives: 10, 13, 30 bottom right; ShutterStock, Inc./Ng Yin Jian: 21, 30 bottom left; Superstock, Inc.: 22, 30 top right (Michael Rutherford), 17.